Igor Sukhin

# Chess Camp

## Volume 7: Opening Tactics

MONGOOSE
*Press*

Publisher: Mongoose Press
1005 Boylston Street, Suite 324
Newton Highlands, MA 02461
info@mongoosepress.com
www.MongoosePress.com
ISBN: 978-1-936277-30-8   1-936277-30-1
Library of Congress Control Number: 2010932524
Distributed to the trade by National Book Network
custserv@nbnbooks.com, 800-462-6420
For all other sales inquiries please contact the publisher.

Editor: Jorge Amador
Typesetting: Frisco Del Rosario
Cover Design: Al Dianov
First English edition
0 987654321

# Contents

# Note for Coaches, Parents, Teachers, and Trainers

By this point in the *Chess Camp* series, the student has acquired experience in solving problems to master both typical tactical techniques for gaining a material advantage (the double attack, discovered check, and so on) and defensive methods (escaping from attack, counterattacking, etc.). In previous volumes, the material was grouped by theme.

Now the student must use his or her acquired skills in conditions where the theme of the attacking or defensive maneuver is unknown. This corresponds more closely to the reality of a chess game, in which you don't immediately know which specific aspect of the position will be the defining one (a pin; the poor position of a piece; something else). Students themselves must carefully analyze the positions that have been created, get a feel for their peculiarities, and work out which specific method of play needs to be used to win material or defend the position.

The contents of this book are classified by opening type. This will help the beginning player to familiarize himself with the fundamental tactical ideas that are characteristic of a particular opening, as well as with some patterns to be found in the treasure trove of the chess arts. The tactical blows most commonly encountered in the games of beginners are presented with a greater number of examples (in different openings) than are other, rarely encountered tactical ideas.

The examples include both very simple, one-move problems and positions in which a beautiful maneuver will not be found right away. Some attention has been given to rare opening systems, such as openings where the queen comes into the game early. These kinds of positions occur frequently in the games of inexperienced players, but they are not always given the amount of attention they deserve in the vast chess literature.

When solving the problems in which a defensive maneuver needs to be found, above all the student must see the threat itself (check, double attack, etc.), and — based on that — start to look for the best defensive move (or maneuver). This defensive idea may be: 1) a counterattack in which you manage to defend and to acquire a material advantage; 2) a defense that preserves material equality; 3) a defense in a difficult position, when even after the defensive maneuver your opponent's position remains preferable (but a quick loss is likely if you fail to find the best move).

5

# Silly Games
## Copycat (mirror-image) games

Wanting to take the game to a draw, Black is copying White's moves. Punish him!
**White to move.** Win the queen.

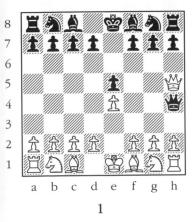

1

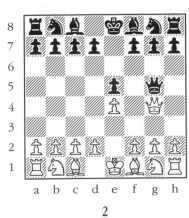

2

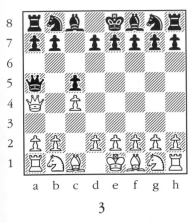

3

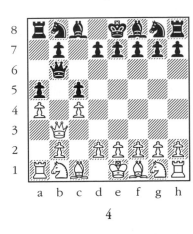

4

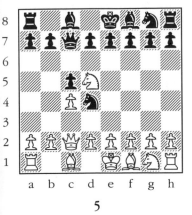

5

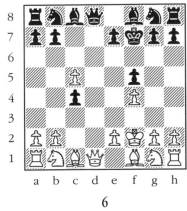

6

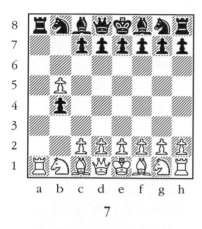

7

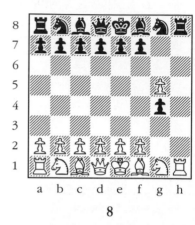

8

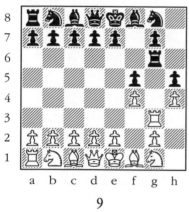

9

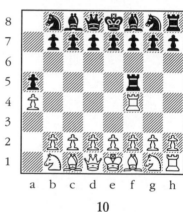

10

11

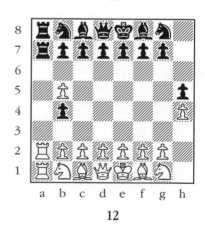

12

**White to move.** Win a knight.

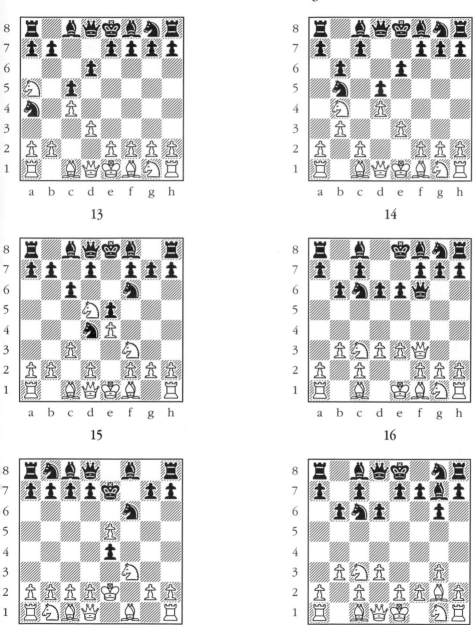

13

14

15

16

17

18

9

**White to move.** Win a bishop.

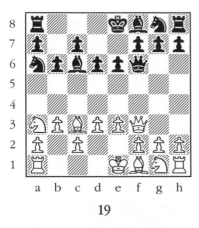

19

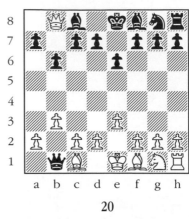

20

21

22

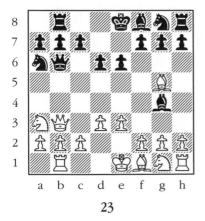

23

24

# Silly Games
## Winning a piece on moves 2-4 of the game

**Black to move.** Win the queen on the second move of the game.

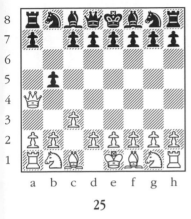

25

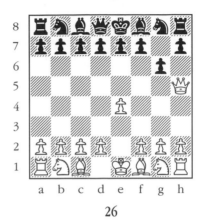

26

27

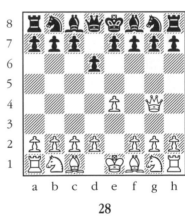

28

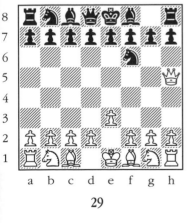

29

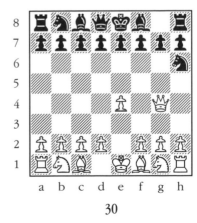

30

**Black to move.** Win a bishop on the second move of the game.

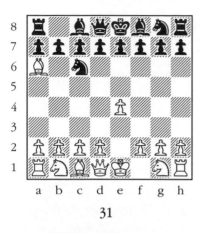

31

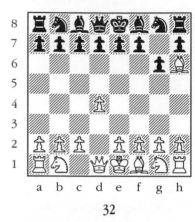

32

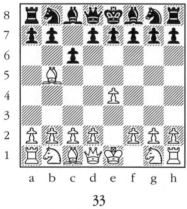

33

34

35

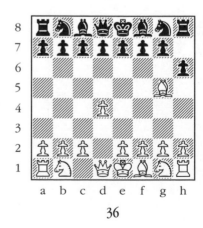

36

**Black to move.** Win a knight on the second move of the game.

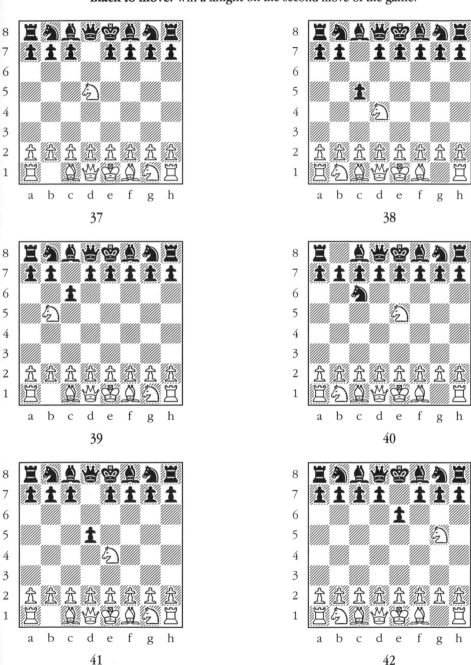

37

38

39

40

41

42

13

**White to move.** Win a pawn on the second move of the game.

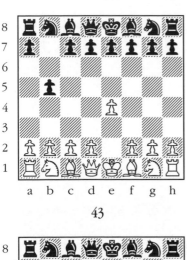

43

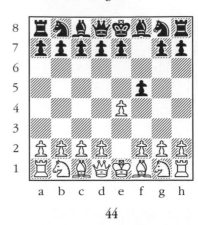

44

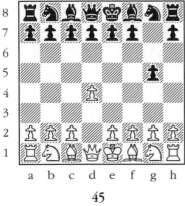

45

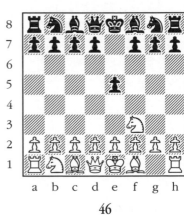

46

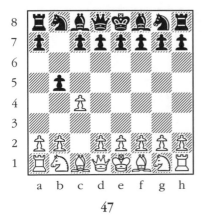

47

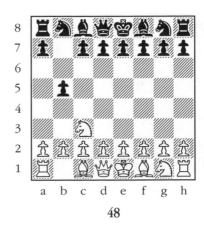

48

14

**Black to move.** Win the exchange or a pawn on the second move of the game.

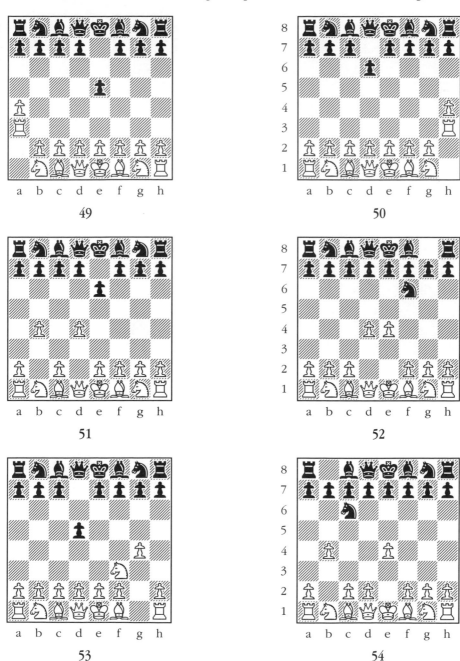

49

50

51

52

53

54

15

**White to move.** Win a rook on the third move of the game.

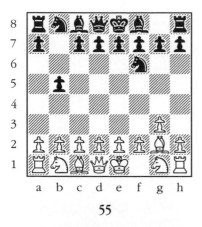

55

56

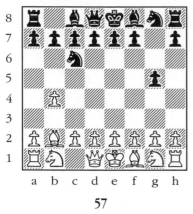

57

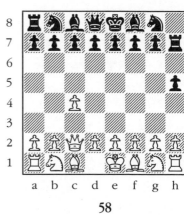

58

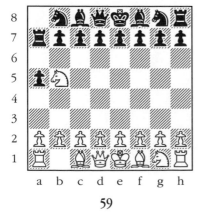

59

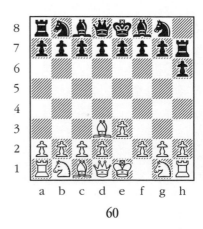

60

**Black to move.** Win the queen on the third move of the game.

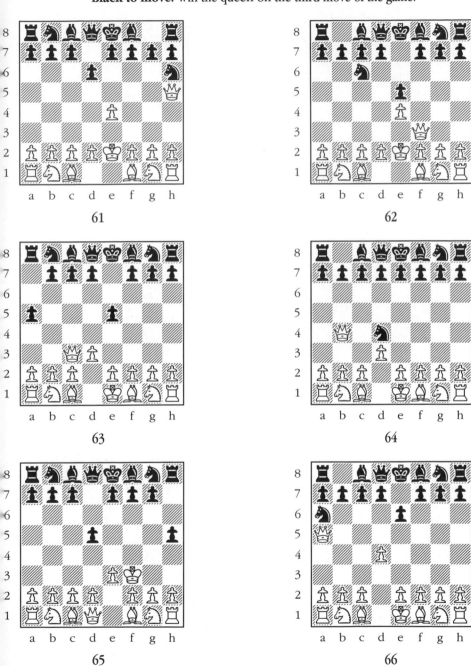

61

62

63

64

65

66

17

**Black to move.** Win the queen on the fourth move of the game.

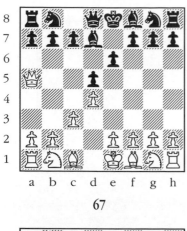

67

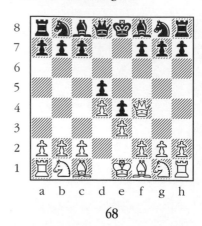

68

69

70

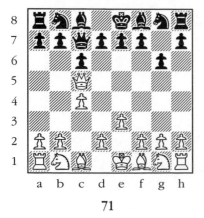

71

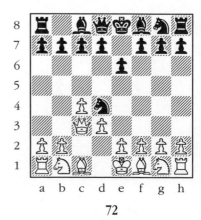

72

# Winning Material in the Open Games
## The opening variation 1. e4 e5 2. ♛h5

**Black to move.** Find the best continuation.

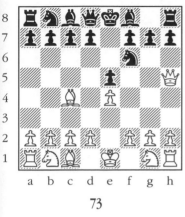

73

74

75

76

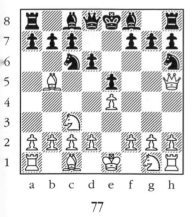

77

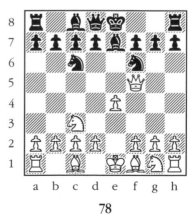

78

# The opening variation 1. e4 e5 2. ♕h5

**White to move.** Find the best continuation.

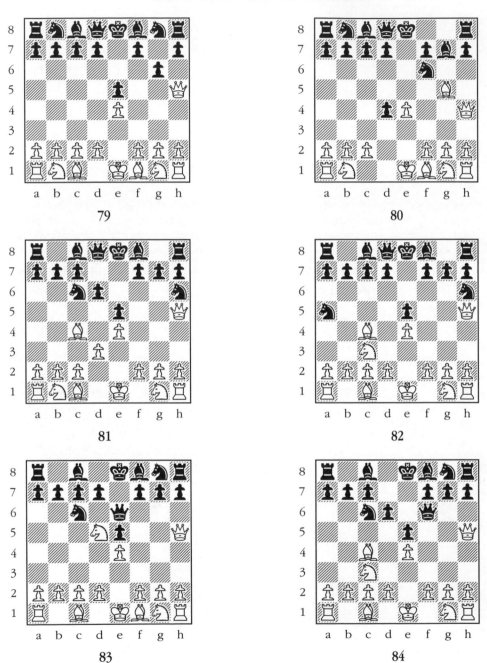

79

80

81

82

83

84

# King's Gambit
## 1. e4 e5 2. f4

**White to move.** Find the best continuation.

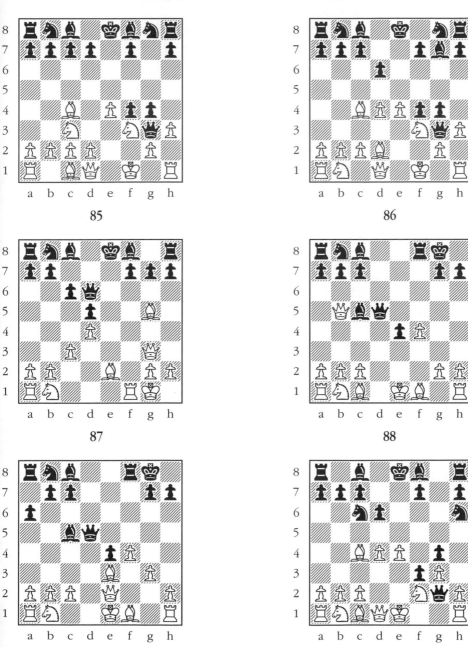

85

86

87

88

89

90

# King's Gambit

## 1. e4 e5 2. f4

**Black to move.** Find the best continuation.

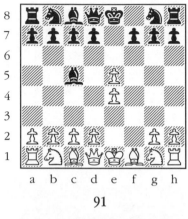

91

92

93

94

95

96

# Center Game

## 1. e4 e5 2. d4

**White to move.** Find the best continuation.

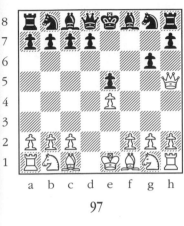

97

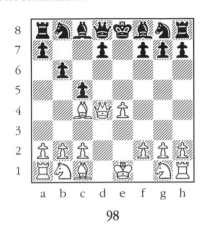

98

99

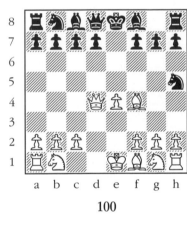

100

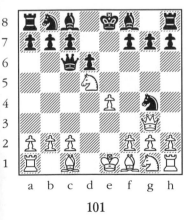

101

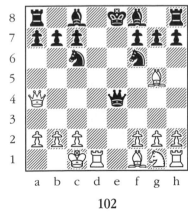

102

# Center Game
## 1. e4 e5 2. d4

**Black to move.** Find the best continuation.

103

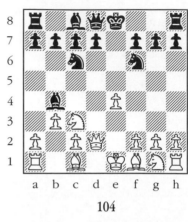

104

105

106

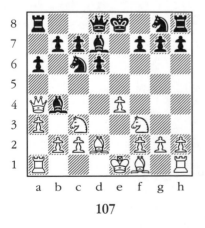

107

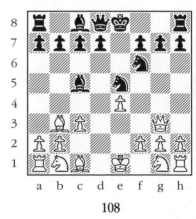

108

# Danish Gambit

## 1. e4 e5 2. d4 cxd4 3. c3

**White to move.** Find the best continuation.

109

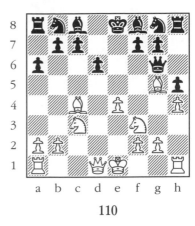

110

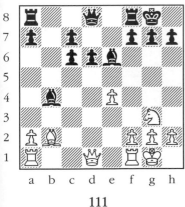

111

112

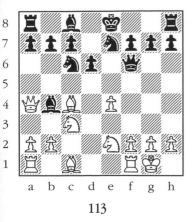

113

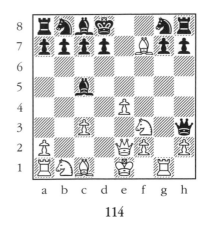

114

# Bishop's Opening
## 1. e4 e5 2. ♗c4

**White to move.** Find the best continuation.

115

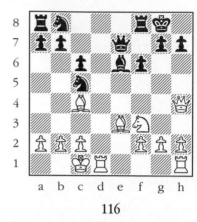

116

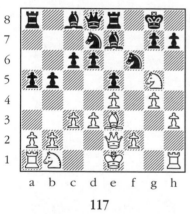

117

118

119

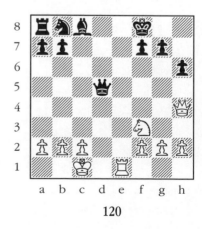

120

# Bishop's Opening

## 1. e4 e5 2. ♗c4

**Black to move.** Find the best continuation.

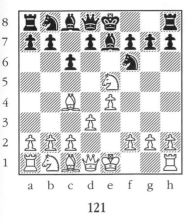

121

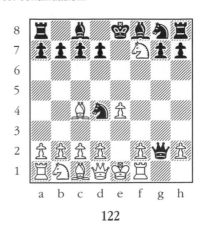

122

123

124

125

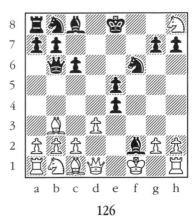

126

# Vienna Game

## 1. e4 e5 2. ♘c3

**White to move.** Find the best continuation.

127

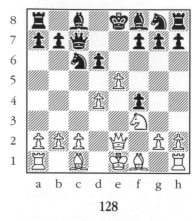

128

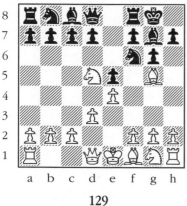

129

130

131

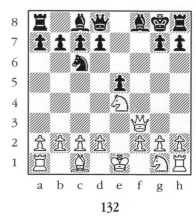

132

# Damiano's Defense

## 1. e4 e5 2. ♘f3 f6

**White to move.** Find the best continuation.

133

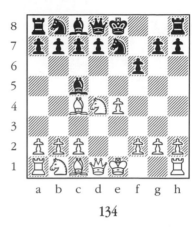

134

135

136

137

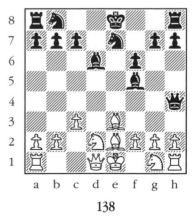

138

# The opening variation 1. e4 e5 2. ♘f3 ♕f6

**White to move.** Find the best continuation.

139

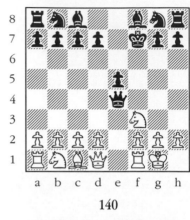

140

141

142

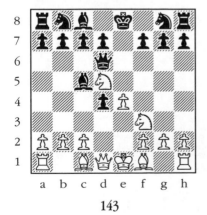

143

144

# Latvian Gambit

## 1. e4 e5 2. ♘f3 f5

**White to move.** Find the best continuation.

145

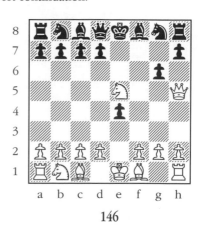

146

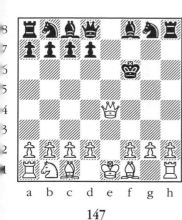

147

148

149

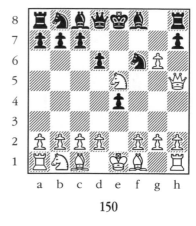

150

# Latvian Gambit

## 1. e4 e5 2. ♘f3 f5

**Black to move.** Find the best continuation.

151

152

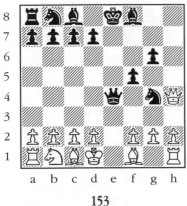

153

154

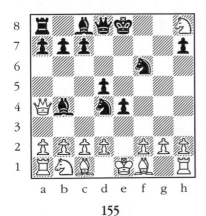

155

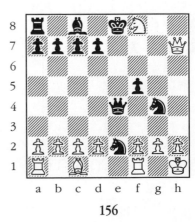

156

# Philidor's Defense
## 1. e4 e5 2. ♘f3 d6

**White to move.** Find the best continuation.

157

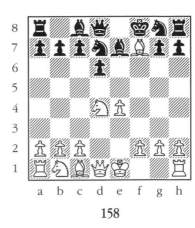

158

159

160

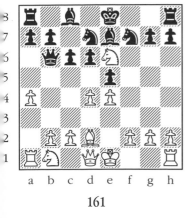

161

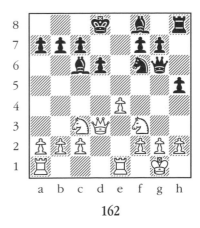

162

# Philidor's Defense
## 1. e4 e5 2. ♘f3 d6

**Black to move.** Find the best continuation.

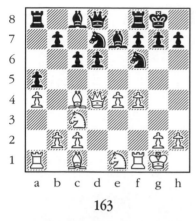

163

164

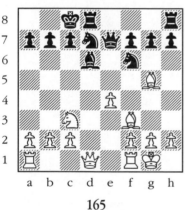

165

166

167

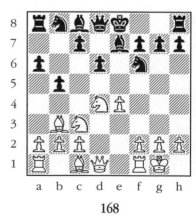

168

# The opening variation 1. e4 e5 2. ♘f3 ♗d6

**White to move.** Find the best continuation.

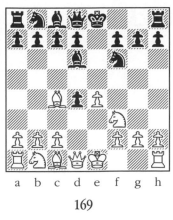

169

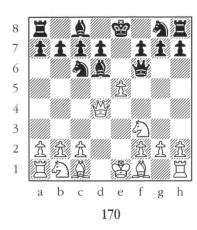

170

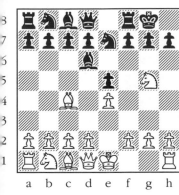

171

172

173

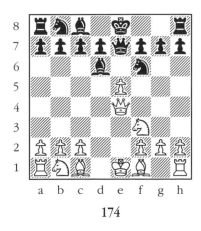

174

# Petroff's Defense

## 1. e4 e5 2. ♘f3 ♘f6

**White to move.** Find the best continuation.

175

176

177

178

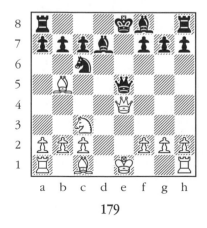

179

180

# Petroff's Defense

## 1. e4 e5 2. ♘f3 ♘f6

**Black to move.** Find the best continuation.

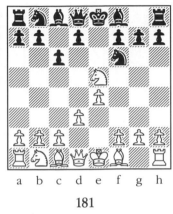

181

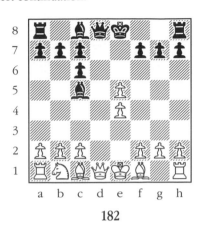

182

183

184

185

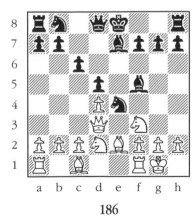

186

# Scotch Game
## 1. e4 e5 2. ♘f3 ♘c6 3. d4

**White to move.** Find the best continuation.

187

188

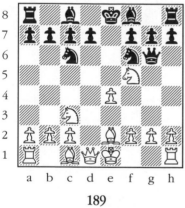

189

190

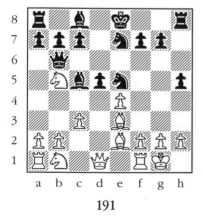

191

192

# Göring Gambit

## 1. e4 e5 2. ♘f3 ♘c6 3. d4 cxd4 4. c3

**White to move.** Find the best continuation.

193

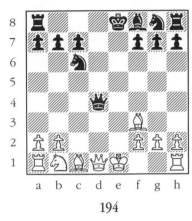

194

195

196

197

198

# Two Knights' Defense
## 1. e4 e5 2. ♘f3 ♘c6 3. ♗c4 ♘f6

**White to move.** Find the best continuation.

199

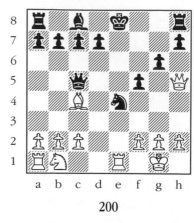

200

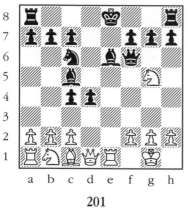

201

202

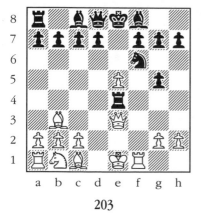

203

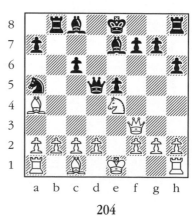

204

# Two Knights' Defense

## 1. e4 e5 2. ♘f3 ♘c6 3. ♗c4 ♘f6

**Black to move.** Find the best continuation.

205

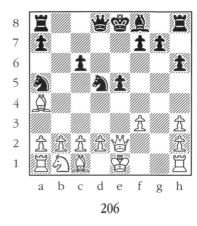

206

207

208

209

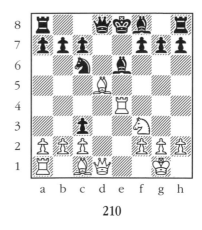

210

# Four Knights' Game

## 1. e4 e5 2. ♘f3 ♘c6 3. ♘c3 ♘f6

**White to move.** Find the best continuation.

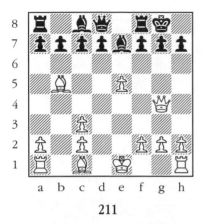

211

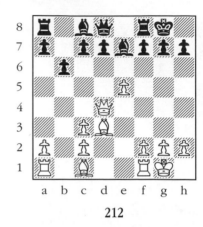

212

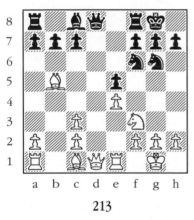

213

214

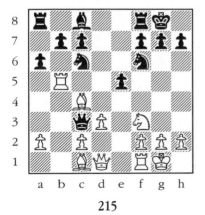

215

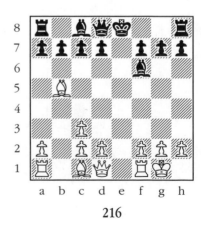

216

# Four Knights' Game

## 1. e4 e5 2. ♘f3 ♘c6 3. ♘c3 ♘f6

**Black to move.** Find the best continuation.

217

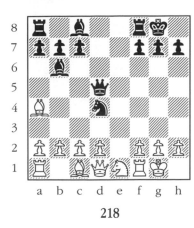

218

219

220

221

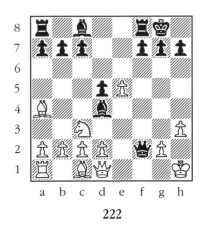

222

# Giuoco Piano

## 1. e4 e5 2. ♘f3 ♘c6 3. ♗c4 ♗c5

**White to move.** Find the best continuation.

223

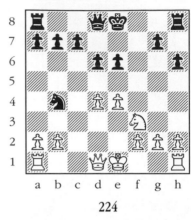

224

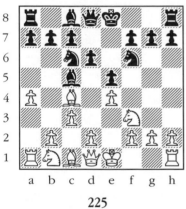

225

226

227

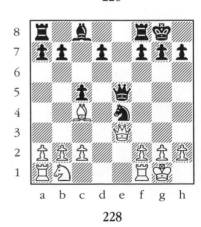

228

# Giuoco Piano

## 1. e4 e5 2. ♘f3 ♘c6 3. ♗c4 ♗c5

**Black to move.** Find the best continuation.

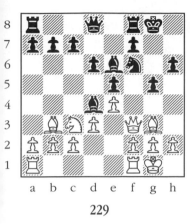

229

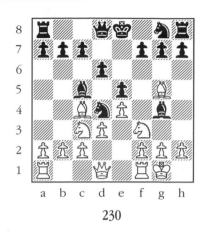

230

231

232

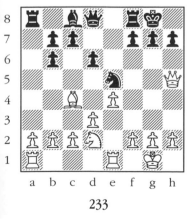

233

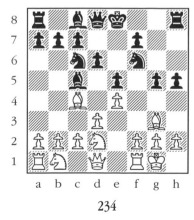

234

# Evans Gambit

## 1. e4 e5 2. ♘f3 ♘c6 3. ♗c4 ♗c5 4. b4

**White to move.** Find the best continuation.

235

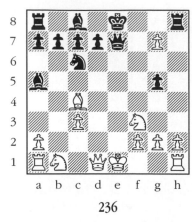

236

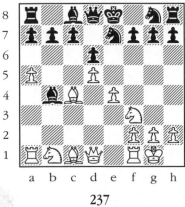

237

238

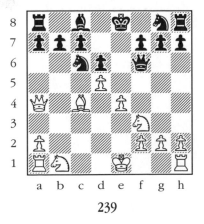

239

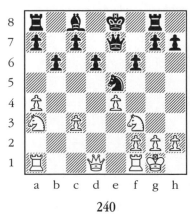

240

# Ruy López

## 1. e4 e5 2. ♘f3 ♘c6 3. ♗b5

**White to move.** Find the best continuation.

241

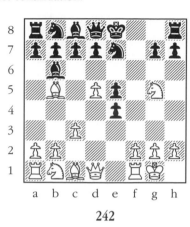

242

243

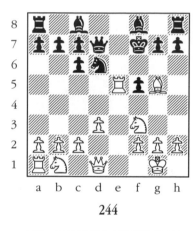

244

245

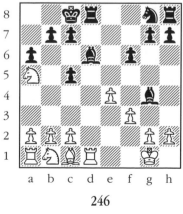

246

# Ruy López

## 1. e4 e5 2. ♘f3 ♘c6 3. ♗b5

**Black to move.** Find the best continuation.

247

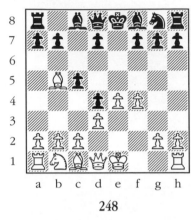

248

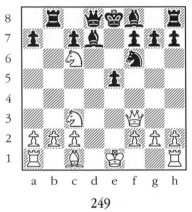

249

250

251

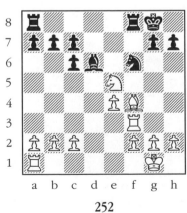

252

# Ruy López
## 1. e4 e5 2. ♘f3 ♘c6 3. ♗b5

**White to move.** Find the best continuation.

253

254

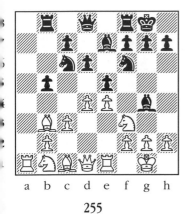

255

256

257

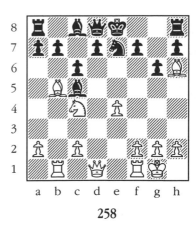

258

# Winning Material in the Semi-Open Games
## Scandinavian Defense 1. e4 d5

**White to move.** Find the best continuation.

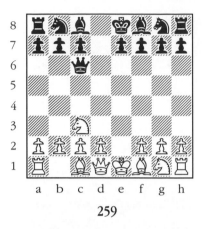

259

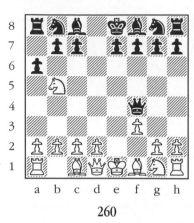

260

261

262

263

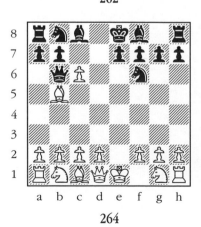

264

# Scandinavian Defense

## 1. e4 d5

**Black to move.** Find the best continuation.

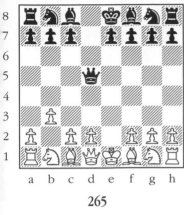

265

266

267

268

269

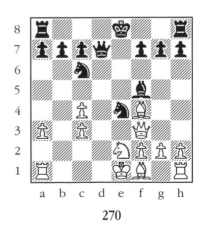

270

# Sicilian Defense

## 1. e4 c5

**White to move.** Find the best continuation.

271

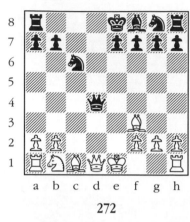

272

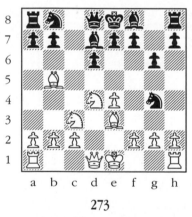

273

274

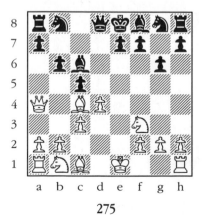

275

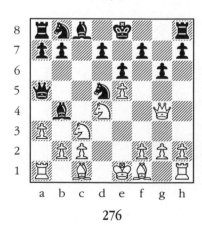

276

# Sicilian Defense

## 1. e4 c5

**Black to move.** Find the best continuation.

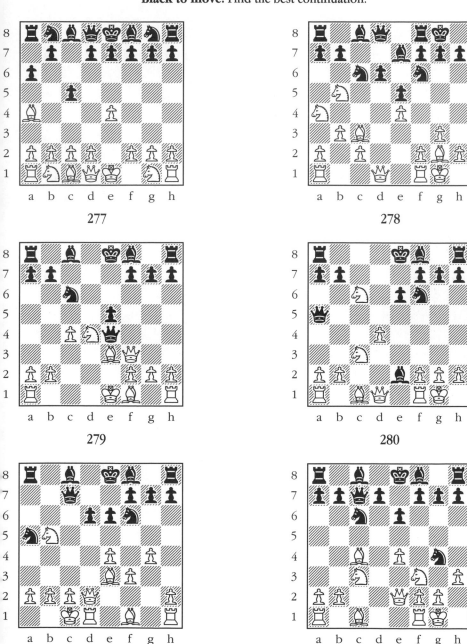

277

278

279

280

281

282

# Sicilian Defense

## 1. e4 c5

**White to move.** Find the best continuation.

283

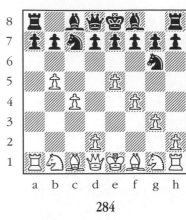

284

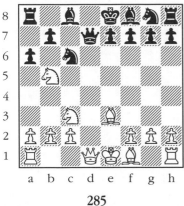

285

286

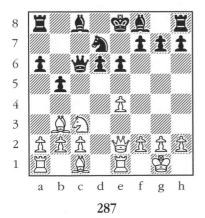

287

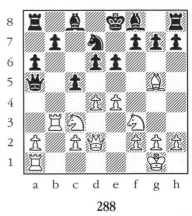

288

# Sicilian Defense

## 1. e4 c5

**Black to move.** Find the best continuation.

289

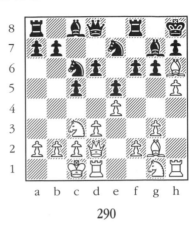

290

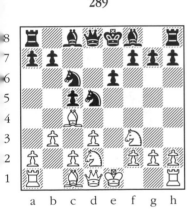

291

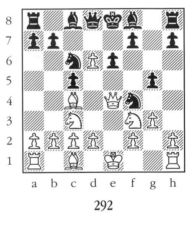

292

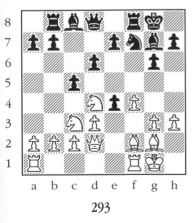

293

294

# Sicilian Defense

## 1. e4 c5

**White to move.** Find the best continuation.

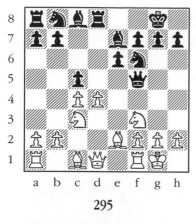

295

296

297

298

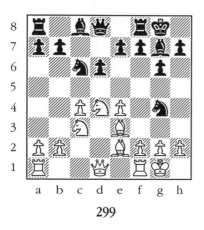

299

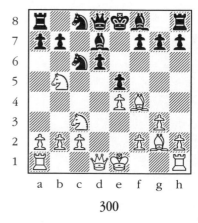

300

# French Defense

## 1. e4 e6

**White to move.** Find the best continuation.

301

302

303

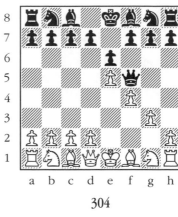

304

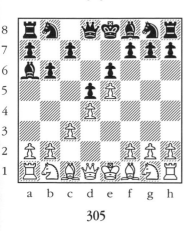

305

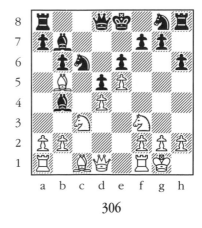

306

# French Defense

## 1. e4 e6

**Black to move.** Find the best continuation.

307

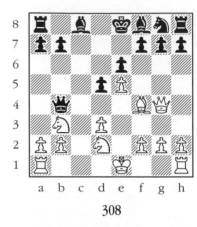

308

309

310

311

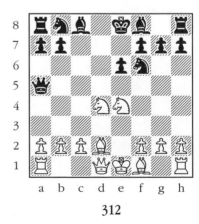

312

# French Defense

## 1. e4 e6

White to move. Find the best continuation.

313

314

315

316

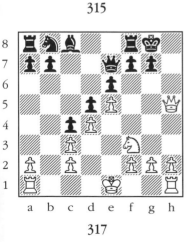

317

318

59

# Caro-Kann Defense

## 1. e4 c6

**White to move.** Find the best continuation.

319

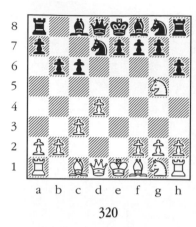

320

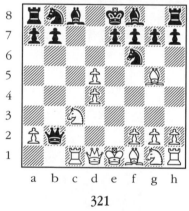

321

322

323

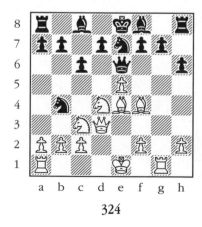

324

# Caro-Kann Defense
## 1. e4 c6

**Black to move.** Find the best continuation.

325

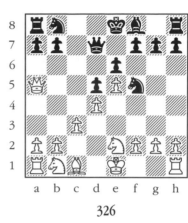

326

327

328

329

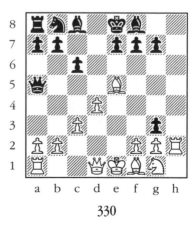

330

# Pirc Defense

## 1. e4 d6

**White to move.** Find the best continuation.

331

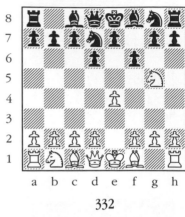

332

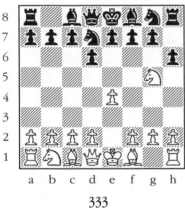

333

334

335

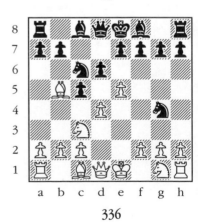

336

# Pirc Defense

## 1. e4 d6

**Black to move.** Find the best continuation.

337

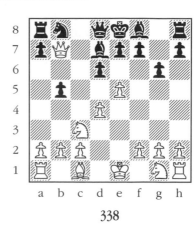

338

339

340

341

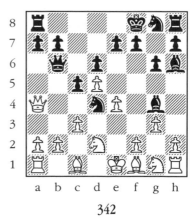

342

# Owen's Defense

## 1. e4 b6

**White to move.** Find the best continuation.

343

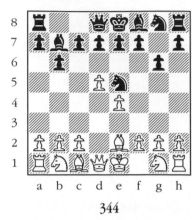

344

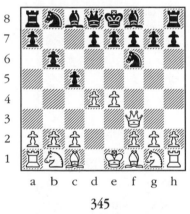

345

346

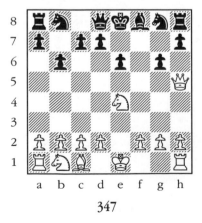

347

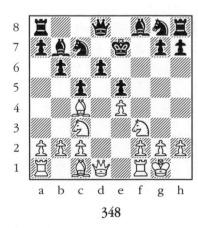

348

# Owen's Defense

## 1. e4 b6

**Black to move.** Find the best continuation.

349

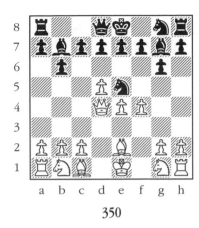

350

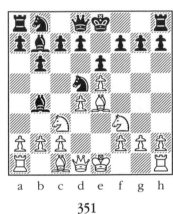

351

352

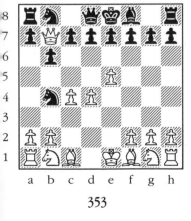

353

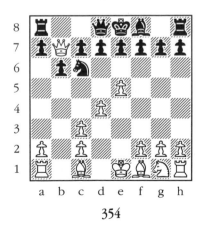

354

# Alekhine's Defense

## 1. e4 ♘f6

**White to move.** Find the best continuation.

355

356

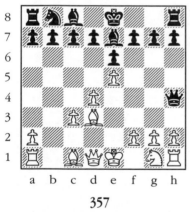

357

358

359

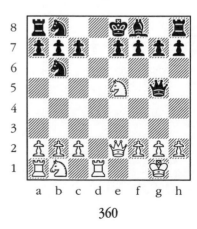

360

# Alekhine's Defense

## 1. e4 ♞f6

**Black to move.** Find the best continuation.

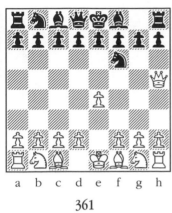

361

362

363

364

365

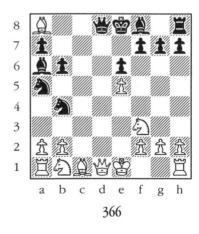

366

# Winning Material in the Closed Games

## Bird's Opening 1. f4

**Black to move.** Find the best continuation.

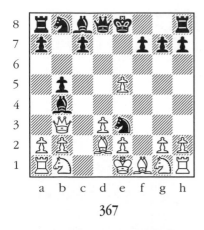

367

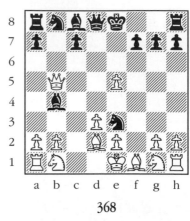

368

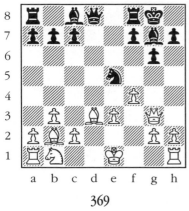

369

370

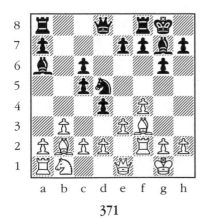

371

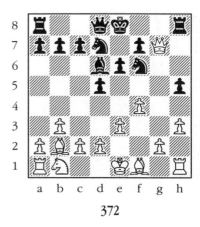

372

# From's Gambit

## 1. f4 e5

**Black to move.** Find the best continuation.

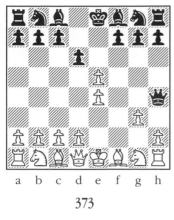

373

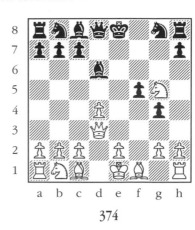

374

375

376

377

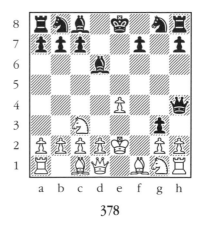

378

# Orangutan Opening

## 1. b4

**White to move.** Find the best continuation.

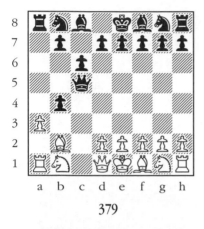

379

380

381

382

383

384

# Orangutan Opening

## 1. b4

**Black to move.** Find the best continuation.

385

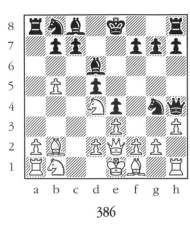

386

387

388

389

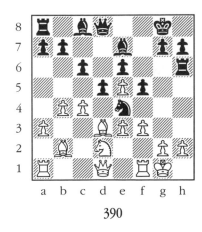

390

# English Opening

## 1. c4

**White to move.** Find the best continuation.

391

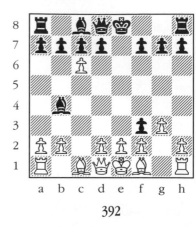

392

393

394

395

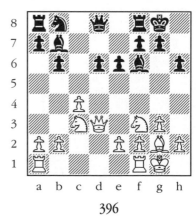

396

# English Opening

## 1. c4

**Black to move.** Find the best continuation.

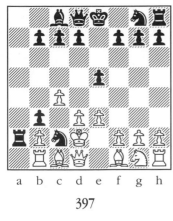

397

398

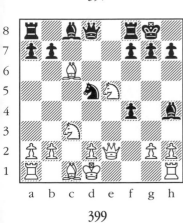

399

400

401

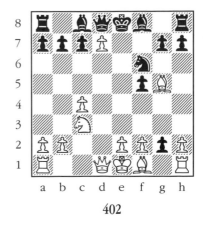

402

# Réti's Opening

## 1. ♘f3

**White to move.** Find the best continuation.

403

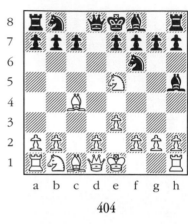

404

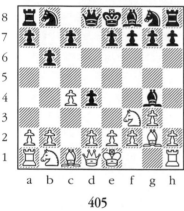

405

406

407

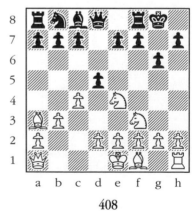

408

# Réti's Opening

## 1. ♘f3

**Black to move.** Find the best continuation.

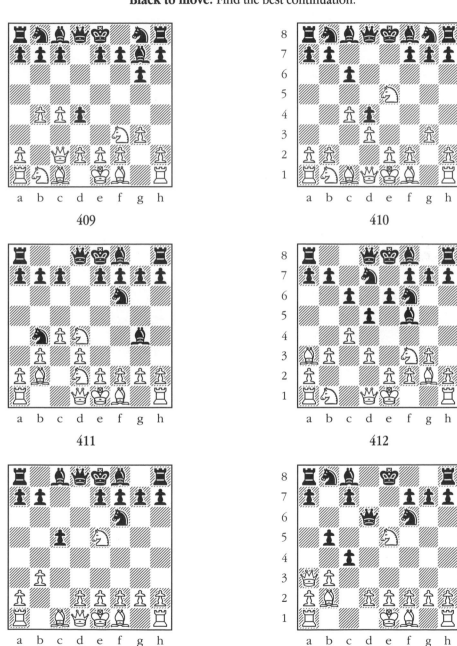

409

410

411

412

413

414

# Queen's Pawn Opening

## 1. d4

**White to move.** Find the best continuation.

415

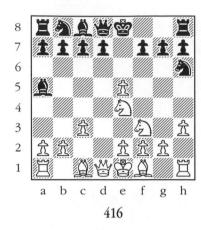

416

417

418

419

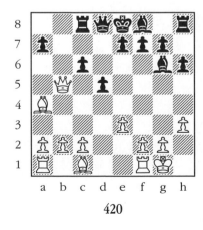

420

# Queen's Pawn Opening

## 1. d4

**Black to move.** Find the best continuation.

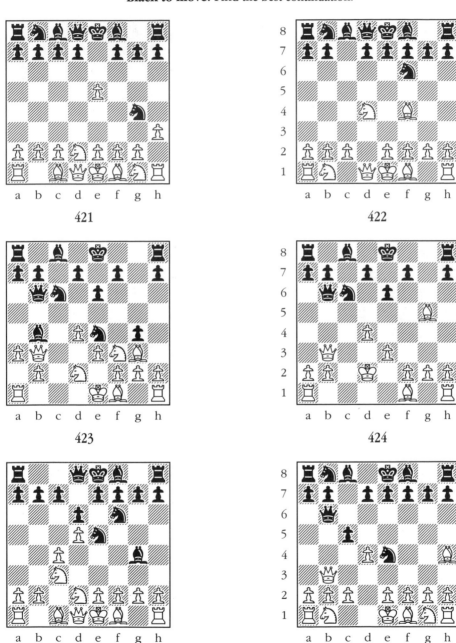

421

422

423

424

425

426

# Dutch Defense

## 1. d4 f5

**White to move.** Find the best continuation.

427

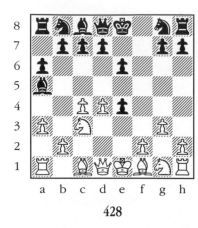

428

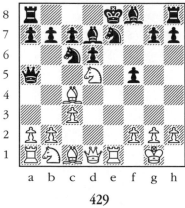

429

430

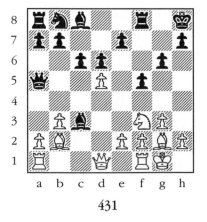

431

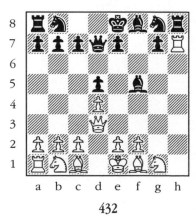

432

# Dutch Defense

## 1. d4 f5

**Black to move.** Find the best continuation.

433

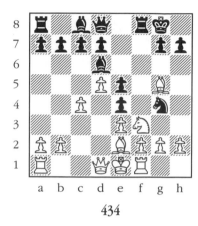

434

435

436

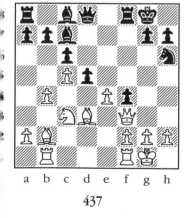

437

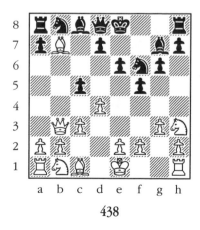

438

# Queen's Gambit

## 1. d4 d5 2. c4

**White to move.** Find the best continuation.

439

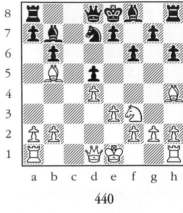

440

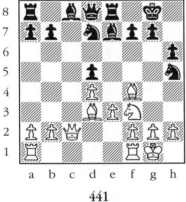

441

442

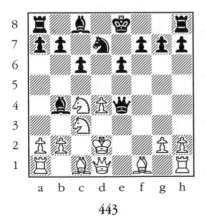

443

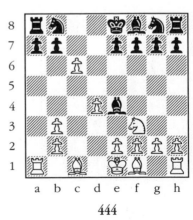

444

# Queen's Gambit
## 1. d4 d5 2. c4

**Black to move.** Find the best continuation.

445

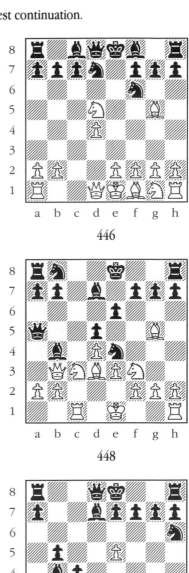

446

447

448

449

450

# Albin Countergambit
## 1. d4 d5 2. c4 e5

**White to move.** Find the best continuation.

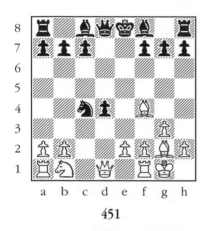

451

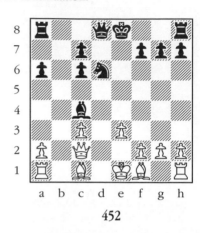

452

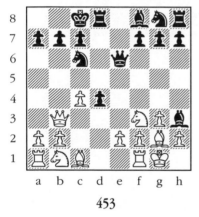

453

454

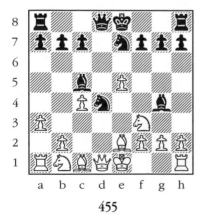

455

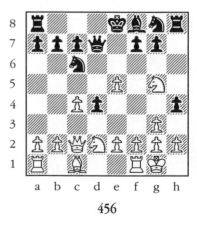

456

# Albin Countergambit

## 1. d4 d5 2. c4 e5

**Black to move.** Find the best continuation.

457

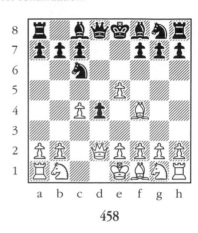

458

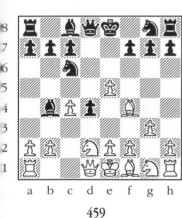

459

460

461

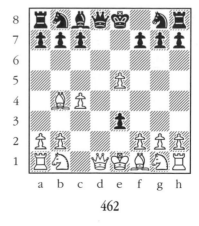

462

# Budapest Gambit
## 1. d4 ♘f6 2. c4 e5

**White to move.** Find the best continuation.

463

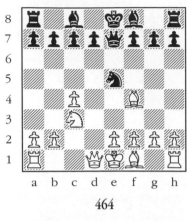

464

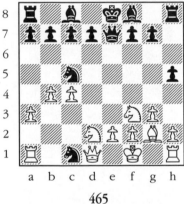

465

466

467

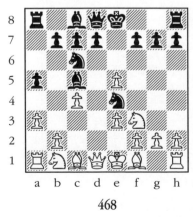

468

# Budapest Gambit
## 1. d4 ♘f6 2. c4 e5

**Black to move.** Find the best continuation.

469

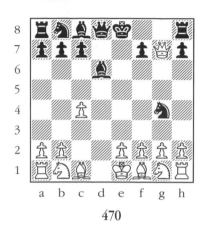

470

471

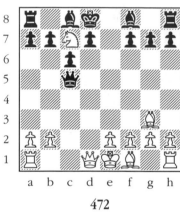

472

473

474

# Grünfeld Defense
## 1. d4 ♞f6 2. c4 g6 3. ♞c3 d5

**White to move.** Find the best continuation.

475

476

477

478

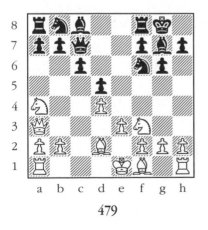

479

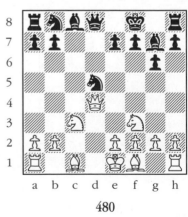

480

# Grünfeld Defense
## 1. d4 ♞f6 2. c4 g6 3. ♞c3 d5

**Black to move.** Find the best continuation.

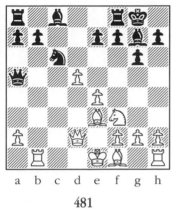

481

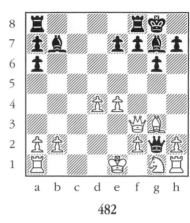

482

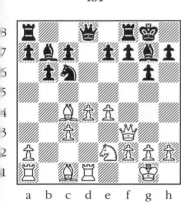

483

484

485

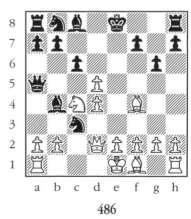

486

# King's Indian Defense

## 1. d4 ♘f6 2. c4 g6 3. ♘c3 ♗g7

**White to move.** Find the best continuation.

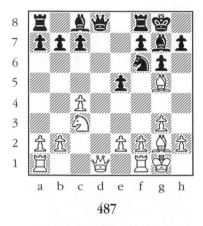

487

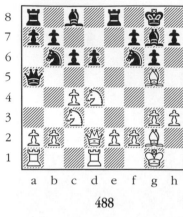

488

489

490

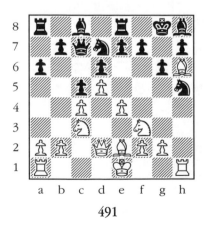

491

492

# King's Indian Defense

## 1. d4 ♘f6 2. c4 g6 3. ♘c3 ♗g7

**Black to move.** Find the best continuation.

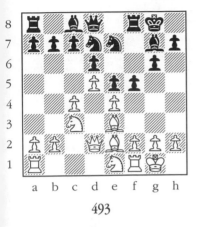

493

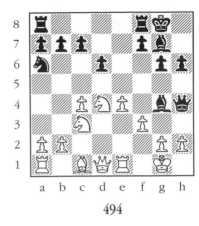

494

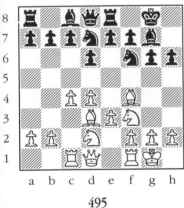

495

496

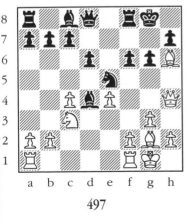

497

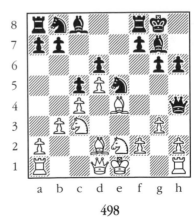

498

89

# Queen's Indian Defense

## 1. d4 ♞f6 2. c4 e6 3. ♞f3 b6

**White to move.** Find the best continuation.

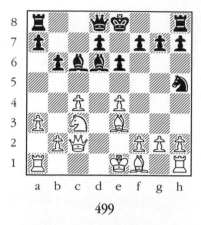

499

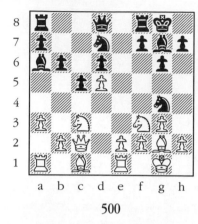

500

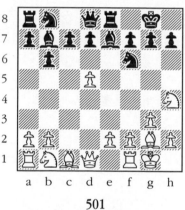

501

502

503

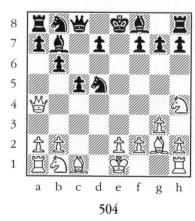

504

# Nimzo-Indian Defense

## 1. d4 ♘f6 2. c4 e6 3. ♘c3 ♗b4

**Black to move.** Find the best continuation.

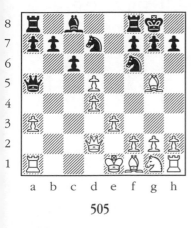

505

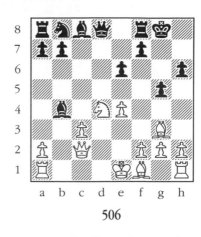

506

507

508

509

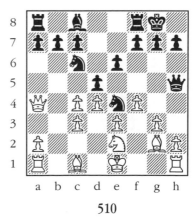

510

# Defending in the Opening
## Defending in the Closed Games
## Positions 2-3 moves into the game

**White to move.** Find the best move.

511

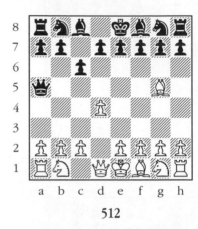

512

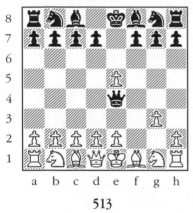

513

514

515

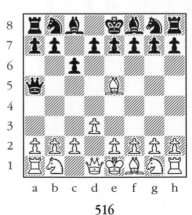

516

# Positions 2-3 moves into the game

**Black to move.** Find the best move.

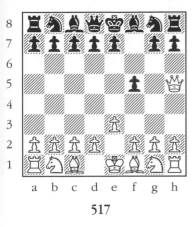

517

518

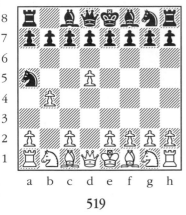

519

520

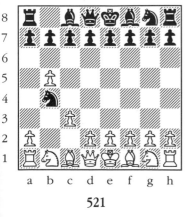

521

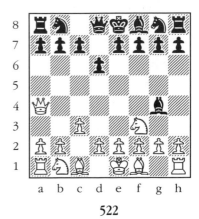

522

# Positions 4 moves into the game

**White to move.** Find the best move.

523

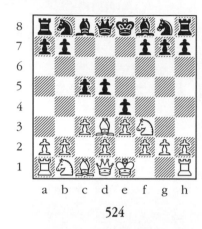

524

525

526

527

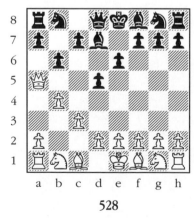

528

# Positions 4 moves into the game

**Black to move.** Find the best move.

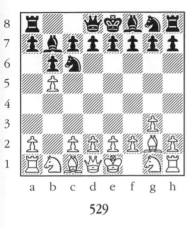

529

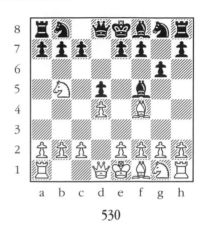

530

531

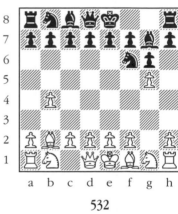

532

533

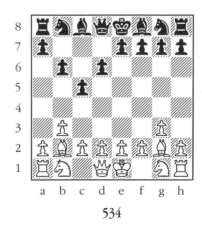

534

# Positions 4-5 moves into the game

**White to move.** Find the best move.

535

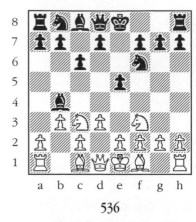

536

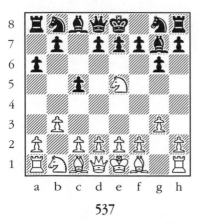

537

538

539

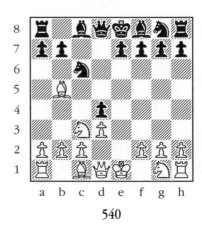

540

# Positions 5-6 moves into the game

**Black to move.** Find the best move.

541

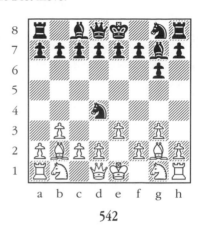

542

543

544

545

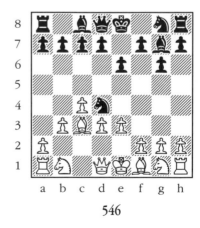

546

# Defending in the Semi-Open Games

## Positions 3 moves into the game

**White to move.** Find the best move.

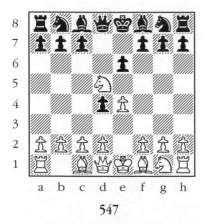

547

548

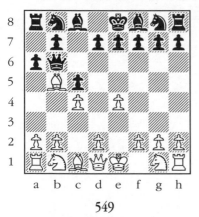

549

550

551

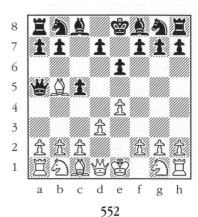

552

# Positions 2-3 moves into the game

**Black to move.** Find the best move.

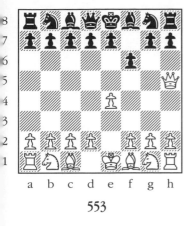

553

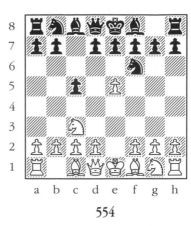

554

555

556

557

558

# Positions 3-4 moves into the game

**White to move.** Find the best move.

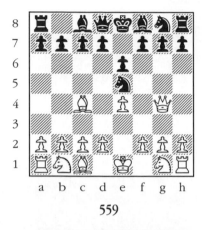

559

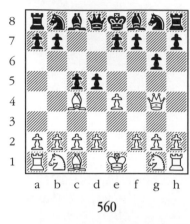

560

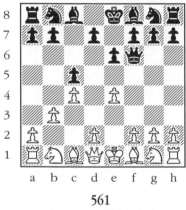

561

562

563

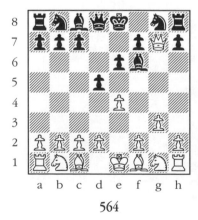

564

# Positions 4 moves into the game

**Black to move.** Find the best move.

565

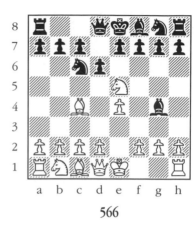

566

567

568

569

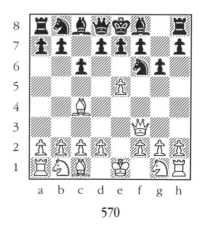

570

# Positions 4 moves into the game

**White to move.** Find the best move.

571

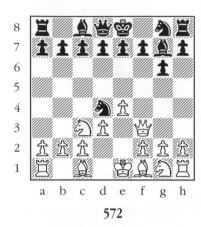

572

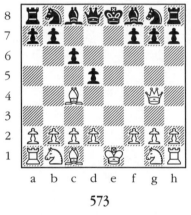

573

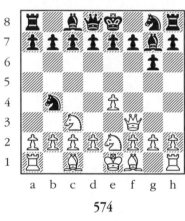

574

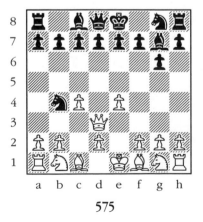

575

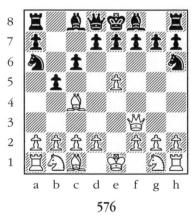

576

# Positions 5-6 moves into the game

**Black to move.** Find the best move.

577

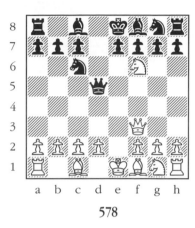

578

579

580

581

582

# Defending in the Open Games

## Positions 3 moves into the game

**White to move.** Find the best move.

583

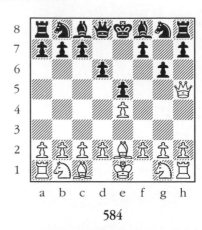

584

585

586

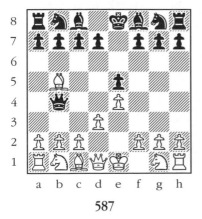

587

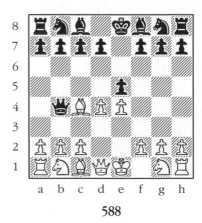

588

# Positions 3-4 moves into the game

**Black to move.** Find the best move.

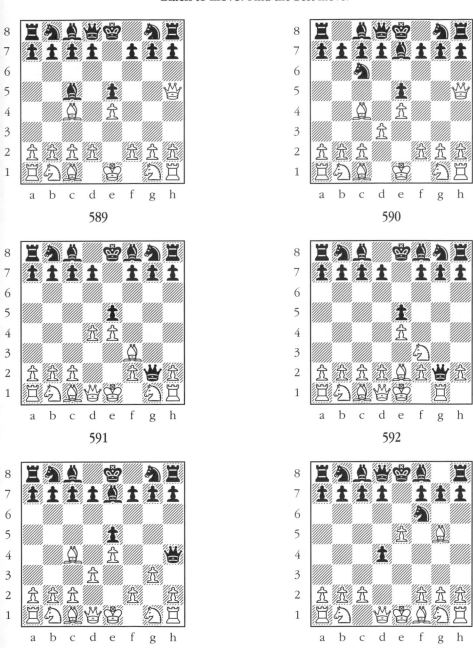

589

590

591

592

593

594

# Positions 3-4 moves into the game

**White to move.** Find the best move.

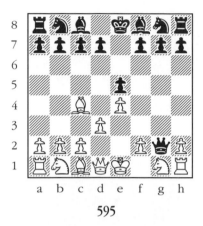

595

596

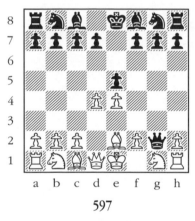

597

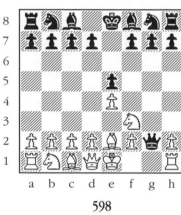

598

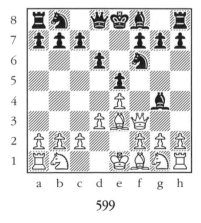

599

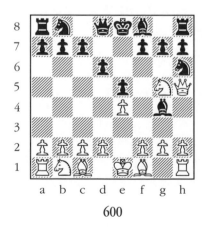

600

# Positions 5-6 moves into the game

**Black to move.** Find the best move.

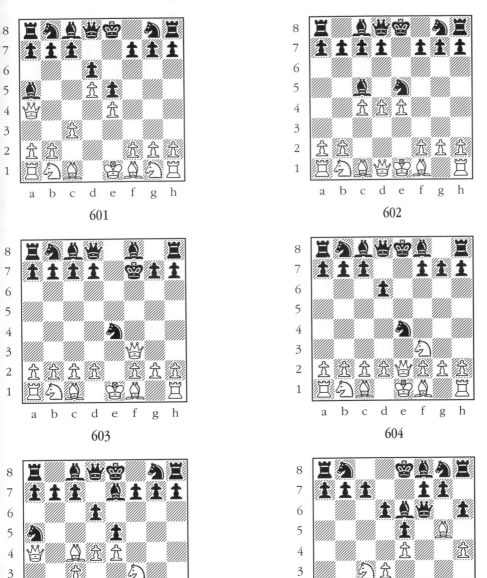

601

602

603

604

605

606

# Positions 5-6 moves into the game

**White to move.** Find the best move.

607

608

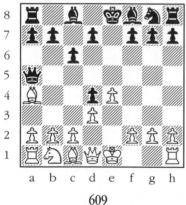

609

610

611

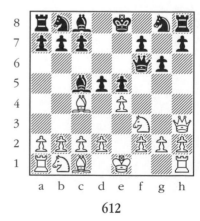

612

# Positions 7-8 moves into the game

**Black to move.** Find the best move.

613

614

615

616

617

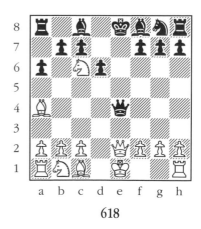

618

# Solutions

1. 1. ♕xh4.

2. 1. ♕xg5.

3. 1. ♕xa5.

4. 1. ♕xb6.

5. 1. ♘xc7+.

6. 1. ♕xd8.

7. 1. ♖xa8.

8. 1. ♖xh8.

9. 1. ♖xg6.

10. 1. ♖xf5.

11. 1. ♖xe5.

12. 1. ♖xa7.

13. 1. ♕xa4+.

14. 1. ♗xb5+.

15. 1. ♘xf6+ and 2. cxd4.

16. 1. ♕xc6+.

17. 1. exf6+.

18. 1. ♗xc6+.

19. 1. ♕xc6+.

20. 1. ♕xc8+.

21. 1. ♗xc6+.

22. 1. ♗xb5+.

23. 1. ♕a4+ and 2. ♕xg4.

24. 1. ♕h5+ and 2. ♕xc5.

25. 1...bxa4.

26. 1...gxh5.

27. 1... ♖xh5.

28. 1...♗xg4.

29. 1...♘xh5.

30. 1...♘xg4.

31. 1...bxa6.

32. 1...♗(♘)xh6.

33. 1...cxb5.

34. 1...exf4.

35. 1...dxc4.

36. 1...hxg5.

37. 1...♕xd5.

38. 1...cxd4.

39. 1...cxb5.

40. 1...♘xe5.

41. 1...dxe4.

42. 1...♕xg5.

43. 1. ♗xb5.

44. 1. exf5.

45. 1. ♗xg5.

46. 1. ♘xe5.

47. 1. cxb5.

48. 1. ♘xb5.

49. 1...♗xa3.

50. 1...♗xh3.

51. 1...♗xb4+.

52. 1...♘xe4.

53. 1...♗xg4.

54. 1...♘xb4.

55. 1. ♗xa8.

56. 1. ♕xa8.

57. 1. ♗xh8.

58. 1. ♕xh7.

59. 1. ♘xa7.

60. 1. ♗xh7.

61. 1...♗g4+.

62. 1...♘d4+.

63. 1...♗b4.

64. 1...♘xc2+.

65. 1...♗g4+.

66. 1...♗b4+.

67. 1...b6.

68. 1...♗d6.

69. 1...♘f6.

70. 1...b5.

71. 1...e5.

72. 1...♗b4 2. ♕xb4 ♘c2+.

73. 1...♘xh5.

74. 1...g6.

75. 1...d5.

76. 1...g6.

77. 1...♗g4.

78. 1...♘d4 and 2... ♘xc2+.

79. 1. ♕xe5+ and 2. ♕xh8.

80. 1. e5.

81. 1. ♗xh6, and if 1... gxh6 then 2. ♕xf7#.

82. 1. ♕xe5+.

83. 1. ♘xc7+.

84. 1. ♘d5 ♕d8 2. ♘b6 g6 3. ♕f3.

85. 1. ♘e2.

86. 1. ♗e1.

87. 1. ♗f4 ♕e7 2. ♗xb8, when 2...♕xe2 3. ♖e1 is good for White.

88. 1. ♗c4.

89. 1. ♕c4.

90. 1. ♗f1.

91. 1...♕h4+ 2. g3 (2. ♔e2 ♕xe4#) 2... ♕xe4+.

92. 1...g2+ 2. ♘xh4 gxh1♕.

93. 1...♗e6, and 2. ♘h4 ♗xh4+.

94. 1...♗a4.

95. 1...♕e7 2. d4 (2. ♘f3 ♕xe4#) 2...d6.

96. 1...♗f6 2. ♕g3 ♗h4.

97. 1. ♕xe5+.

98. 1. ♕d5.

99. 1. f4.

100. 1. ♕e5+.

101. 1. ♗b5 ♕xb5 2. ♘xc7+.

102. 1. ♖d8+ ♔xd8 2. ♕xe4.

103. 1...♗b4.

104. 1...♘xe4.

105. 1...♘f3+.

106. 1...♕f6.

107. 1...♘d4 2. ♕xb4 ♘xc2+.

108. 1...♗xf2+ 2. ♕xf2 (2. ♔xf2 ♘xe4+) 2...♘d3+.

109. 1. ♗g5, and if 1...♕f5(g6) then 2. ♕d8#.

110. 1. ♘e5, when 1... dxe5 2. ♕d8# and 1.. ♕h7 2. ♗xf7# win for White.

111. 1. ♕d4.

112. 1. exf6.

113. 1. ♘d5 ♘xd5 2. exd5.

114. 1. ♖g3.

115. 1. dxe5+ ♕xe5 2. ♗f4.

116. 1. ♗xc5.

117. 1. ♘e6.

118. 1. ♕xd6, and if 1...cxd6 then 2. ♗xf7#.

119. 1. ♕xf7+ ♔xf7 2. dxc6+, with the idea of 3. cxb7 and 4. bxa8♕.

120. 1. ♖d1.

121. 1...♕a5+.

122. 1...♕xe4+, and if 2. ♗e2 then 2...♘f3#.

123. 1...♗b4+ 2. c3 ♕xd4.

124. 1...♗xc3.

125. 1...a6.

126. 1...♗g4 2. ♕d2 ·3, and if 3. ♔c3 e2#.

127. 1. c3.

128. 1. exd6+.

129. 1. ♕f3.

130. 1. a3 ♗a5 2. ♗d2.

131. 1. ♕e2+, when both 1...♘e7 2. ♘f6# and 1...♗e7 2. ♘f6+ ♔f8 3. ♗h6# are good for White.

132. 1. ♘g5, and if 1...♕xg5 then 2. ♕d5#.

133. 1. ♕xe5+.

134. 1. ♕h5+.

135. 1. ♕d5.

136. 1. ♗h5.

137. 1. d4, threatening 2. ♗c4+.

138. 1. g3.

139. 1. ♘xc7+.

140. 1. ♘g5+.

141. 1. ♘xf6+.

142. 1. ♖xe5+.

143. 1. ♗f4 with the idea of 2. ♘xc7+.

144. 1. ♗b5 ♕xb5 2. ♘xc7+.

145. 1. ♘f7+.

146. 1. ♘xg6.

147. 1. ♕d4+.

148. 1. ♘e6+.

149. 1. ♘g6+.

150. 1. g7+.

151. 1...♘xc2+.

152. 1...♘xf2+.

153. 1...♘e3+.

154. 1...♖g4 2. ♕h3 ♖xe4+.

155. 1...♗d7 2. ♕xb4 ♘xc2+.

156. 1...♘f4, and White has to give up his queen, as 2. f3 ♕e2 doesn't save him.

157. 1. ♘d5.

158. 1. ♘e6+.

159. 1. ♗g5.

160. 1. ♗b5.

161. 1. a5 ♕xb2 2. ♗c3.

162. 1. ♘e5 ♕h7 2. ♘xf7+.

163. 1...d5 with the idea of 2...♗c5.

164. 1...a6.

165. 1...♕e5.

166. 1...♘b6 2. ♕xd8 ♖xd8.

167. 1...♘c5 2. ♗xf7+ (2. ♕a3 ♘d3) 2...♕xf7.

168. 1...c5 with the idea of 2...c4.

169. 1. e5.

170. 1. exf6.

171. 1. ♕h5 h6 2. ♘xf7, and ♗lack must give up the exchange, as 2...♕e8 3. ♘xh6+ leads to a quick mate.

172. 1. ♕d5 ♗b4+ (1...d6 2. ♕xf7+ ♔d7 3. ♕xg7) 2. c3.

173. 1. ♕d5, and 1... ♘c6 2. ♕xf7#.

174. 1. ♕e2.

175. 1. ♘c6+.

176. 1. c3 dxc3 2. bxc3.

177. 1. g4.

178. 1. ♕e2 ♕e7 (1...d5 2. d3) 2. ♘d5.

179. 1. ♗xc6.

180. 1. ♘e6+.

181. 1...♕a5+.

182. 1...♗xf2+ 2. ♔e2 ♗g4+.

183. 1...♗c5.

184. 1...♗f6.

185. 1...♗b7 2. ♕xa7 ♗c5.

186. 1...♘g3.

187. 1. ♘xc6 bxc6 2. ♗xc5.

188. 1. a5.

189. 1. ♘h4.

190. 1. ♘xc6.

191. 1. ♗xc5 ♕xc5 2. ♕d4 ♕xd4 3. cxd4.

192. 1. 0-0-0+.

193. 1. ♕d5.

194. 1. ♗xc6+.

195. 1. ♕h5 h6 2. ♘xf7.

196. 1. ♘xd5 ♘xf3++ 2. ♔f1.

197. 1. ♕xd8+ ♔xd8 2. ♘xf7+.

198. 1. ♘xe6, and if 1...♕xe6 then 2. ♘c7#.

199. 1. c7+.

200. 1. ♖xe4+.

201. 1. ♘xe6 fxe6 2. ♕h5+.

202. 1. ♘h4 with the idea of 2. ♘f6+.

203. 1. ♗xf7+ ♔xf7 (1...♔e7 2. exf6+) 2. ♕xe4.

204. 1. ♘f6+ ♗xf6 2. ♕xd5.

205. 1...♗g4.

206. 1...♕h4+.

207. 1...♗a6+.

208. 1...♗g4.

209. 1...♘e3+.

210. 1...♘e7 (but not 1...♘b4 2. ♗g5 ♕xd5 3. ♖d4).

211. 1. ♗h6 g6 2. ♗xf8.

212. 1. ♕e4.

213. 1. ♗a3.

214. 1. ♘xd4.

215. 1. ♗b2.

216. 1. ♗a3.

217. 1...♗g4, when 2. ♕g3 doesn't save White because of 2...♕xg3.

218. 1...♗c4, and if 2. ♗b3 then 2...♘e2+ 3. ♔h1 ♘g3+.

219. 1...♗xc3+.

220. 1...♗g4, and because of the threat of 2...♕h4 White has to give up his queen.

221. 1...♘c7.

222. 1...♗g4, and it's impossible to play either 2. ♕xg4 ♕g1# or 2. hxg4 ♕h4#.

223. 1. ♘xb6 axb6 2. d5 ♘a5 3. ♗d3 ♗g4 4. b4.

224. 1. ♕a4+ ♘c6 2. d5.

225. 1. b4 ♗b6 2. a5.

226. 1. ♘xb6.

227. 1. ♘d5.

228. 1. ♘c3.

229. 1...♗g4.

230. 1...♗xf3 2. ♗xd8 ♗xd1.

231. 1...♗h3.

232. 1...♗xh3, and White can't play 2. ♕xa8 because of 2...♕g3 followed by mate.

233. 1...♗g4.

234. 1...h4.

235. 1. ♗a3.

236. 1. ♕e2 ♕xe2+ 2. ♔xe2.

237. 1. ♕a4+.

238. 1. ♗xf6 ♕c8 2. ♘xb6 cxb6 3. f3.

239. 1. e5.

240. 1. ♕d5.

241. 1. ♕c4.

242. 1. ♘e6.

243. 1. ♘xe5, when 1...♗xd1 2. ♗xf7# is good for White.

244. 1. ♖e7+ ♗xe7 2. ♘e5+.

245. 1. ♘d5.

246. 1. e5.

247. 1...c6 2. ♘c4 (2. ♗c4 ♕a5+) 2...d5.

248. 1...♕a5+.

249. 1...e4 2. ♘xe4 ♗xc6 3. ♘xf6+ ♕xf6.

250. 1...♘xd4 2. ♕xd4 c5 3. ♕d5 ♗e6 4. ♕c6+ ♗d7 5. ♕d5 c4.

251. 1...♗b4+ 2. c3 ♕xb5.

252. 1...♘h5.

253. 1. ♘xd4 exd4 2. ♖e1 f5 3. f3.

254. 1. ♕e2.

255. 1. d5.

256. 1. ♘xe6 with the idea of 2. ♖xe4.

257. 1. ♗c7, and 1...♕xc7 2. ♕f7+ with mate.

258. 1. ♗d4, and if 1...♗xd4 then 2. ♘d6#.

259. 1. ♗b5.

260. 1. d4 ♕h4+ 2. g3.

261. 1. ♗b5 ♕xb5 2. ♘xc7+.

262. 1. ♘c4 ♕a6 (1...♕b4 2. a3) 2. ♘d6+ ♔d8 3. ♘xf7+.

263. 1. b4 ♕xb5 2. ♘xc7+.

264. 1. cxb7+.

265. 1...♕e5+.

266. 1...♘f6.

267. 1...♗d7+.

268. 1...♗xc3+.

269. 1...♗g6.

270. 1...♘e5, and if 2. ♗xe5 then 2...♕d2#.

271. 1. ♕a4+.

272. 1. ♗xc6+.

273. 1. ♕xg4.

274. 1. ♘e6+.

275. 1. ♘e5, and if 1...♗xa4 then 2. ♗xf7#.

276. 1. axb4 ♕xa1 2. ♘b3.

277. 1...b5 2. ♗b3 c4.

278. 1...a6 2. ♘a3 b5 3. ♘b2 b4.

279. 1...♗b4+ 2. ♔d1 ♗g4.

280. 1...♕xc3.

281. 1...♘b3+ 2. ♔b1 (2. axb3 ♖a1#) 2...♘xd2+.

282. 1...♘d4 2. hxg4 (2. ♘xd4 ♕h2#) 2...♘xe2+.

283. 1. ♗xf7+.

284. 1. f5 ♘xe5 2. d4.

285. 1. ♕xd7+ ♗xd7 (1...♔xd7 2. 0-0-0+) 2. ♘c7+.

286. 1. ♗b6.

287. 1. ♗d5, when 1...exd5 2. exd5+ wins the black queen.

288. 1. ♘d5, and if 1...♕xd2 then 2. ♘c7#.

289. 1...♕e5+.

290. 1...♗xh6, and if 2. ♕xh6 then 2...g5 and 3...♘g8.

291. 1...♘c3.

292. 1...f5 2. ♕xc6+ (2. ♕e3 ♘g2+) 2...bxc6.

293. 1...e3 2. ♗(♕)xe3 cxd4.

294. 1...♗xe4 (1...♘xe4 2. ♗g2 ♖b8 isn't bad either), and if 2. ♘xe4 then 2...♕xc2#.

295. 1. ♘h4.

296. 1. c4.

297. 1. h3 ♘xe5 2. ♘xe5, and 2...dxe5 3. ♗xf7+ wins the black queen.

298. 1. ♘b6 ♕c6 (1...♕xb3 2. axb3) 2. ♘xa8.

299. 1. ♗xg4 ♗xg4 (1...♘xd4 2. ♗xc8; 1...♘xd4 2. ♗xc8 ♗xc3 3. ♗xb7) 2. ♘xc6 ♗xd1 3. ♘xd8.

300. 1. ♘d5 ♗e7 (1...♕a5+ 2. ♗d2) 2. ♘bc7+.

301. 1. e5.

302. 1. e5.

303. 1. e5.

304. 1. ♗d3.

305. 1. ♗xa6 ♘xa6 2. ♕a4+.

306. 1. ♕a4.

307. 1...b5 2. ♗b3 c4.

308. 1...g5 2. ♕xg5 ♗h6.

309. 1...♘xd4, and 2. ♕xd4 ♗c5.

310. 1...axb5 2. ♕xa8 ♘b6 traps the queen.

311. 1...♗b6, and, for example, 2. ♘b3 ♗xf2+ 3. ♔d2 ♕e3#.

312. 1...♕e5.

313. 1. ♗g5.

314. 1. ♗b5+.

315. 1. ♘c6.

316. 1. g4 with the idea of 2. g5.

317. 1. ♘g5, and the threat of mate forces Black to give up his queen.

318. 1. ♗g5 ♗xf3 2. ♕c1 (but not 2. ♕d2 ♗b4) 2...♗b4+ 3. ♔f1, and the threat of mate forces Black to give up his queen.

19. 1. g4 ♗e4 (1... ♗g6 2. h5 ♗e4 3. f3) . f3 ♗g6 3. h5.

20. 1. ♘e6, and 1... xe6 2. ♕h5+.

21. 1. ♘a4.

22. 1. ♖c3.

23. 1. fxe7+ ♔xe7 2. ♗g5+.

24. 1. ♕f1.

25. 1...b5.

26. 1...b6.

27. 1...f5 and 2...f4.

28. 1... ♗xb1, and f 2. ♖xb1 then 2... ♗b4.

29. 1...gxf2+.

30. 1...♕xe5+ 2. xe5 gxh2.

31. 1. ♕a4+.

32. 1. ♘e6.

33. 1. ♘e6, when 1... xe6 2. ♕h5+ leads to heckmate.

34. 1. axb6 ♗xd1 2. ♖xa7.

35. 1. ♕xg4.

36. 1. d5 a6 2. dxc6 xb5 3. cxb7 ♗xb7 4. ♕xg4.

37. 1...b5.

38. 1... ♗c6.

39. 1...♕h4+.

40. 1...♘b3+.

41. 1...♗h6.

42. 1...♕a5, and if 2. ♕xa5 then 2...♘c2#.

43. 1. b4.

44. 1. f4.

45. 1. e5.

46. 1. ♘xf6+.

47. 1. ♕e5.

348. 1. ♗xg8, threatening 2. ♗g5+.

349. 1...♗xg2.

350. 1...♘f3+.

351. 1...♗xc3+ (1... ♘xc3 2. bxc3 ♗xc3+ 3. ♗d2 is weaker) 2. bxc3 ♘xc3.

352. 1...♘f6 and 2... ♗xg2.

353. 1...♘8c6 2. ♘a3 (2. a3 ♘c2+ 3. ♔d1 ♘xa1) 2...♖b8.

354. 1...a6 2. e6 (2. d5 ♘a5; 2. ♗xa6 ♖b8) 2...♖a7.

355. 1. e5.

356. 1. f3.

357. 1. g3.

358. 1. ♗g6+.

359. 1. ♕xd5 ♕xd5 2. ♘xc7+.

360. 1. ♖d8+ ♔xd8 2. ♘xf7+.

361. 1...♘xh5.

362. 1...♕h4+ 2. ♔e2 (2. g3 ♘xg3) 2... ♘g3+ 3. hxg3 ♕xh1.

363. 1...♕xd4.

364. 1...b5.

365. 1...♘xe4, and if 2. ♗xd8 ♗xf2+ 3. ♔e2 ♘d4#.

366. 1...♘d3+.

367. 1...♗e6 2. ♕xb4 ♘c2+.

368. 1...♗d7.

369. 1...♘xd3+.

370. 1...♕xd3 threatening 2...♕d1#.

371. 1...dxe3.

372. 1... ♖g8 2. ♕h6 ♗f8.

373. 1...♕xe4+.

374. 1...h6.

375. 1...♖xh4, and if 2. gxh4 then 2... ♕xh4#.

376. 1...♖xh2 (1... ♘xh2 2. e4 is weaker) 2. ♖xh2 ♘xh2.

377. 1...♘e3.

378. 1...♖xh2.

379. 1. axb4.

380. 1. ♗e5.

381. 1. ♗xg7.

382. 1. ♕xg6+.

383. 1. ♗f7+, and 1... ♔xf7 then 2. e6+.

384. 1. ♖xc8 ♕xc8 2. ♘d6+.

385. 1...♕e5+.

386. 1...♘xf2, and if 2. ♕xf2 then 2...♗g3.

387. 1...♕xc1+.

388. 1...♖xa1.

389. 1...♕xa3 2. ♕xa3 ♘c2+.

390. 1...♘xd2 2. ♕xd2 dxc4.

391. 1. ♗xg8 ♖xg8 2. ♕c4.

392. 1. ♕b3 ♕e7 2. a3.

393. 1. ♘c7+ ♔d8 2. ♗g5+.

394. 1. e3 ♘f5 (1... ♘b5 2. ♕a4) 2. ♕g4.

395. 1. ♗h3.

396. 1. ♘g5 ♗xg5 (1...♗xg2 2. ♕h7#) 2. ♗xb7.

397. 1...♘a3 2. ♕xb3 ♘xb1+.

398. 1...♘g4, and if 2. ♕xg4 then 2...♕d4#.

399. 1...♘e3+.

400. 1...♕xc3+.

401. 1...♖xa4 2. bxa4 ♗b4.

402. 1...♘xd7 2. ♗xg2 (2. ♗xd8 gxh1♕) 2...♕xg5.

403. 1. e4 ♗xe4 2. ♕a4+.

404. 1. ♕xh5, and if 1...♘xh5 then 2. ♗xf7#.

405. 1. ♘e5.

406. 1. ♕a4+.

407. 1. ♘f6+.

408. 1. ♗xe7 ♕xe7 2. ♘f6+ ♕xf6 (2...♔h8 3. ♘xd5+) 3. ♕xf6.

409. 1...d3.

410. 1...♕a5+.

411. 1...♘xd3+.

412. 1...♗xa3 2. ♘xa3 ♕a5+.

413. 1...♕d4.

414. 1...c3 2. ♕xd6 cxd6.

415. 1. ♘c4.

416. 1. ♗g5 f6 2. exf6 ♘f7 3. fxg7.

417. 1. ♘xd6+ exd6 2. ♗b5+.

418. 1. ♖a1 ♕b2 2. ♗c3.

419. 1. ♕d5.

420. 1. ♕xc6+.

421. 1...♘e3, and 2. fxe3 ♕h4+.

422. 1...e5, and if 2. ♗xe5 then 2...♕a5+.

423. 1...♘xd2 (2. ♘xd2 ♗xd2+).

424. 1...♕a5+.

425. 1...♘d3+.

426. 1...♕h6 2. ♕e3 (2...♕c1# was threatened) 2...♕xh4.

427. 1. b4 ♗b6 2. c5.

428. 1. ♕h5+.

429. 1. b4.

430. 1. ♕h5 with the idea of 2. ♘g6#.

431. 1. ♕d2(e1).

432. 1. ♗h3.

433. 1...♘e8 threatening 1...♕xa4 and 1...♘f3++.

434. 1...exf3 2. ♗xd8 ♗b4+.

435. 1...e5 2. dxe5 ♗f5.

436. 1...♖xf3, when 2. gxf3 ♕g5+ 3. ♔h1 ♕g4(h5) is good for Black.

437. 1...♗g4.

438. 1...c4 2. ♕b4 (2. ♕b5 a6) 2...♗f8.

439. 1. ♕f3.

440. 1. ♘e5, threatening 2. ♕h5+.

441. 1. ♗c7.

442. 1. ♕xb4.

443. 1. ♘d6+ ♗xd6 2. ♘xe4.

444. 1. ♖xa7, and if 1...♖xa7 then 2. c7.

445. 1...♗b4+ with the idea of 2...♕xc4.

446. 1...♘xd5 2. ♗xd8 ♗b4+.

447. 1...♕xf6 2. ♗xf6 ♗b4+.

448. 1...♗a4.

449. 1...d4 with the idea of 2...♗b4.

450. 1...♗g4, and if 2. hxg4 ♕d3#.

451. 1. ♕a4+.

452. 1. ♗xc4 ♘xc4 2. ♕e4+.

453. 1. ♘g5.

454. 1. ♘e5, and if 1...♘xe5 then 2. ♕xb7#.

455. 1. ♘xd4 ♕xd4 (1...♗xe2 2. ♕a4+) 2. ♕xd4 ♗xd4 3. ♗xg4.

456. 1. e6 fxe6 2. ♕g6+ ♔d8 (2...♔e7 3. ♕f7+ is even worse) 3. ♘f7+.

457. 1...♕xd4.

458. 1...♗b4.

459. 1...g5 2. a3 ♗e7.

460. 1...♗b4+, and if 2. ♔e2 then 2...♕e4#.

461. 1...♕xg5 2. ♘xc6 (2. ♘xg5 ♗b4+) 2...♗xf3.

462. 1...exf2+ 2. ♔e2 fxg1♘+ 3. ♔e1 ♕h4+.

463. 1. b4 ♗b6 2. c5.

464. 1. ♘d5 ♕d6 2. c5.

465. 1. bxc5.

466. 1. ♖a(f)e1.

467. 1. e4.

468. 1. ♕d5 f5 2. exf6.

469. 1...♗b4+.

470. 1...♗e5 2. ♕g5 ♕xg5 3. ♗xg5 ♗xb2.

471. 1...♗b4.

472. 1...♕a5+ 2. ♕d2 ♗b4.

473. 1...♗a4.

474. 1...♘c5.

475. 1. ♗e5.

476. 1. ♗h6 ♘c6 (1...♖e8 2. ♗b5; 1...♘xc3 2. ♖d3) 2. ♗xf8.

477. 1. ♖a5.

478. 1. ♖b3 ♕a4 2. ♗b5.

479. 1. ♘b6 axb6 (1...♕xb6 2. ♗a5) 2. ♕xa8.

480. 1. ♗h6 (1. ♕xd5 ♗xc3+ is bad for White).

481. 1...♗c3.

482. 1...♗xe4.

483. 1...♘e5, and if 2. dxe5 then 2...♕xd1#.

484. 1...♕g4 2. ♗e7 ♗xe2.

485. 1...a5 2. ♕xe7 (2. ♕a3 b4) 2...♖e8 3. ♕a3 b4 or 3...♗f8.

486. 1...♕xa2 2. ♖xa2 ♘xa2.

487. 1. ♕xd8 ♖xd8 2. ♘e4 (2. ♘d5 ♖d6 3. ♘xc7 ♖b8) 2...♘xe4 3. ♗xd8.

488. 1. ♗xf6 ♘xc4 (1...♗xf6 2. ♘d5 ♕xd2 3. ♘xf6+) 2. ♕f4.

489. 1. ♗h5 ♖f7 2. ♘xf5.

490. 1. ♗e7, and if 1...♖xe7 then 2. ♘xf6+.

491. 1. ♖xh5, when 1...gxh5 2. ♕g5+ leads to checkmate.

492. 1. ♘d5, and if 1...♕xd2 then 2. ♘xe7#.

493. 1...f4.

494. 1...♗xd4+, and if 2. ♕xd4 then 2...♕xe1#.

495. 1...e5 2. dxe5 dxe5 3. ♗g3 e4.

496. 1...h6 2. ♘gxe4 (2. ♘cxe4 hxg5) 2...♘xe4 3. ♘xe4 ♗xb2.

497. 1...g5 2. ♗xg5 (2. ♕h5 ♗g4) 2...fxg5.

498. 1...♕xe4, and if 2. ♘xe4 then 2...♘f3+ 3. ♔f1 ♗h3#.

499. 1. ♕d1.

500. 1. ♕a4.

501. 1. d6 ♗xg2 2. dxe7 ♕xe7 3. ♔xg2.

502. 1. ♕d5 ♕xd5 (1...♘c6 2. ♕xc6) 2. ♘xe7+.

503. 1. ♘xf7, and if 1...♔xf7 then 2. ♕xe6#.

504. 1. ♕e4+ ♔d8 2. ♘c3 ♘xc3 3. ♕xb7.

505. 1...♕xd2+ 2. ♔xd2 ♘e4+.

506. 1...♕xd4.

507. 1...♖c8.

508. 1...♘d4 2. ♕a4 ♗xc3.

509. 1...♘xe4, and if 2. ♕xe4 then 2...♗f5 traps the queen.

510. 1...♕xe2+ 2. ♔xe2 ♘xc3+.

511. 1. g3.

512. 1. ♕(♗)d2.

513. 1. ♘f3.

514. 1. ♘c3.

515. 1. ♗d2.

516. 1. ♗c3.

517. 1...g6.

518. 1...♘c6.

519. 1...♘c4.

520. 1...♘a6.

521. 1...♘d5.

522. 1...Q(B)d7.

523. 1. Qg3.

524. 1. Bb5+.

525. 1. Qc3.

526. 1. Qh4.

527. 1. Nc3 (1. Qxb4 Nc2+ is bad).

528. 1. Qa3.

529. 1...Na5.

530. 1...Na6.

531. 1...b5.

532. 1...Nh5.

533. 1...Nxe5.

534. 1...d5.

535. 1. Qd2 Qf6 2. 14.

536. 1. Bd2 otherwise White loses a piece, for example, 1. Bb2 Qa5 2. Qd2 Nd5).

537. 1. Bb2 (1. d4 cxd4 and 1. f4 d6 are unfavorable).

538. 1. e3 (1. Qd3 Bg7 is weaker), and if 1...h5 then 2. Be2 or 2. Bd3.

539. 1. Qe2.

540. 1. Bxc6+.

541. 1...Nxc6.

542. 1...Nf3+ and 2... Bxb2.

543. 1...Nc3.

544. 1...axb5 2. Qxa8 Nc2+.

545. 1...Ne6 (1...Nf5 2. g4 Bxb2 3. Qxb2 is bad).

546. 1...Nf5.

547. 1. Nf4.

548. 1. Qd3.

549. 1. Ba4.

550. 1. Nc3.

551. 1. Bxb5+.

552. 1. Nc3.

553. 1...g6.

554. 1...Ng8.

555. 1...Nc5.

556. 1...Nc6.

557. 1...e6 (1...g6 2. Qxc5 is worse).

558. 1...Nf6 (1...f6 2. Qh5# is bad) 2. e5 Nd5.

559. 1. Qe2.

560. 1. Bb5+.

561. 1. Nc3.

562. 1. d4.

563. 1. Qf3.

564. 1. Qg4.

565. 1...Bg4.

566. 1...Nxe5 (1...Bxd1 2. Bxf7# is bad).

567. 1...h6 2. Bh4 g5.

568. 1...c6 (1...Nc6 2. d5 is bad).

569. 1...Bd7 (the correct defense against 2. d5).

570. 1...d5.

571. 1. Qd3.

572. 1. Qd1.

573. 1. Qe2+.

574. 1. Kd1.

575. 1. Qb3.

576. 1. Bxb5.

577. 1...Nfd7.

578. 1...Nxf6.

579. 1...Bxe5 2. Nxe5 Qa5+.

580. 1...Qd8 (1... Qxb5 2. Nc7+ is bad).

581. 1...Bb4 2. Bxb4 (2. Qd2 Qxa1) 2... Qxa1.

582. 1...Bg7 2. gxh7+ (2. Qf5 Nf6 also leads to sharp play) 1...Kf8.

583. 1. Qd1.

584. 1. Qf3.

585. 1. Qd3.

586. 1. Bb3.

587. 1. Nc3.

588. 1. Nd2.

589. 1...Qe7(f6).

590. 1...g6.

591. 1...Qg6.

592. 1...Qh3.

593. 1...Qf6.

594. 1...Qe7 (1...h6 2. exf6 hxg5 3. Qe2+ is bad) 2. Qe2 h6 3. Bh4 g5.

595. 1. Qf3 (after 1. Qh5 Nf6 White still has to move his queen to f3).

596. 1. Ng1 (1. g4 Nf6 is worse).

597. 1. Bf3.

598. 1. Rg1 (1. Rf1 is passive).

599. 1. Qg3.

600. 1. Qh4.

601. 1...c6.

602. 1...Bb4+.

603. 1...Nf6.

604. 1...Qe7 (if, for example, 1...d5, then 2. d3).

605. 1...c6 (1...Nc6 2. d5 is bad).

606. 1...Qg6 (1...hxg5 2. hxg5 Qxg5 3. Rxh8 is worse).

607. 1. Nf3.

608. 1. Nxg5.

609. 1. c3.

610. 1. Qc3 (1. Qd5 Nge7 is bad).

611. 1. Nxd5 Bxh3 2. Nxf6+.

612. 1. Qxc8+.

613. 1...Be7.

614. 1...Nxf3+.

615. 1...Nc6.

616. 1...Qd7.

617. 1...Bxc3+.

618. 1...Qxe2+ 2. Kxe2 Bd7.